I0820864

INTRODUCTION

Your house becomes a home when it is entirely your own place, with items that suit you and show who you are.

Since 1999, Loods 5 has been the place to be in the Netherlands for interior enthusiasts. In 5 inspiring stores with more than 300 brands, thousands of visitors find their own living style every day. Loods 5 is also 1 of the most well-known Dutch interior brands online: on social media, Loods 5 has more than half a million followers. In this photo book, you will find the current interior trends through the eyes of Loods 5.

Take a look and get inspired!

PENELO
The Ideal City
VERSACE
Surf Shacks
BARCELONA
MAILER MONROE STERN

The vacation feeling can be brought home. This is easy when you think in colors. With light sand tones, for example, a wicker side table, large color prints of your own vacation photos, and lots of yellow, you can bring the sun inside, even in the evening. This way, you can feel like you are on vacation in your own home every day.

HOTEL CALIFORNIA

The Ideal City
WOMAN MADE

Surf Shacks
WOMAN MADE
GREAT WOMEN DESIGNERS
PHAIDON
The Ideal City
Exploring Urban Futures
gestalten

ks
surf

The Ideal City
Jane Hall
WOMAN MADE
GREAT WOMEN DESIGNERS

PENELOP

The Ideal City
Exploring Urban Futures
SPACE10 gestalten
WOMAN MADE
GREAT WOMEN DESIGNERS
PHAIDON
Surf Shacks
Surf
In the Mood for Corsica
Here and there are carefully selected furnishings, such as an Italian bathtub from the 17th century, a 19th-century mirror and a reclaimed 1950s Roca washbasin.

WOMAN
MADE

Surf
Shacks
Vol. 2
by Matt Titone

surf

SUN
SUN
SUN

NUDE
Art Escapes
gestalten
ERWIN OLAF
I AM
aperture
BEYOND THE WEST
New Global Architecture
SELECTED WORKS
– the collector's edition –

LOVE
SURF SHACK
SURF SHACK // Laid-Back Living by the Water
gestalten
SURF ODYSSEY
The Culture of Wave Riding

torq

5
CONTINENTAL
GRAND PRIX 4000

LONDON
HIDE AND SEEK
IRIS VAN HERPEN
ROYALS & REBELS
British Fashion
GREAT ESCAPES GREECE
Frida Kahlo
NUDE
VERTICAL LIVING
GREAT WOMEN DESIGNERS
MADE
WIM WENDERS
HKliving lookbook

THE **NEW** *SEVENTIES*

A conversation pit from the 70s, with rugs and cushions and lots of ceramics. Featuring the soft, round shapes used by the provos and hippies back then to rebel against the previous generation. Yet, this interior feels brand new. The fabrics, pastel tones, waves, checkers, and blocks are all completely contemporary.

DAVID HOCKNEY

HELMUT NEWTON

SUNRISE

SUNSET

DAVID HOCKNEY
Petite Places
PALM TREE DESTINATIONS
gestalten
CATWALK

DAVID HOCKNEY
Petite Places
PALM TREE DESTINATIONS
STEFAN RAPPO
NUDE

VERTICAL LIVING
WOMAN MADE
GREAT WOMEN DESIGNERS
WIM WENDERS
INSTANT STORIES
HKliving lookbook

HELMUT NEWTON
NICE STUFF
THEO-BERT POT
OUDOLF
VERTICAL LIVING
WOMAN MADE
WIM WENDERS
INSTANT STORIES
THE CHOCOLATE SPOON
LOUIS VUITTON
CATWALK
Frida Kahlo
Petite Places
DAVID HOCKNEY

LET'S JUMP

This townhouse with high ceilings already has a lot of character and calls for styling with a nod to bygone times. With warm, colorful furniture and accessories lovingly chosen, you can create surprising still lifes in every room. From every chair in the house, you can see something beautiful: you are home.

STAYING *AT* HOME

GROW

PLEASE

never
GROW
UP
POP ART

PLEASE
DAN

LOUIS VUITTON

THE EYE HAS TO TRAVEL

Diana Vreeland

FRANTOI CUTRERA
SICILIA
Olio ExtraVergine di Oliva Siciliano

This style with sand tones, bamboo, and lots of wood transcends all trends and movements. It's minimalism never gets boring. With neutral colors, you stop time and balance the space. The accessories, in the same natural tones, make your home exude timeless luxury.

MINIMAL *CHIC*

Nº12
Objets d'Amsterdam

meraki
meraki

Plastic Fantastic

5

PARKS
BEYOND THE WEST

Japandi Living
Japandi Living
GEOPARKS
IRIS VAN HERPEN
SCULPTING THE SENSES
IRIS VAN HERPEN

GREEN
VIBES

Olive green, lime green, moss green, mint green, bottle green, canal green, apple green, army green, sage. Green is back from never having been away: on the wall or in the furniture and, of course, in plants and flowers. Green gets warmer when combined with wood. And super stylish with black metal.

LOODS
5

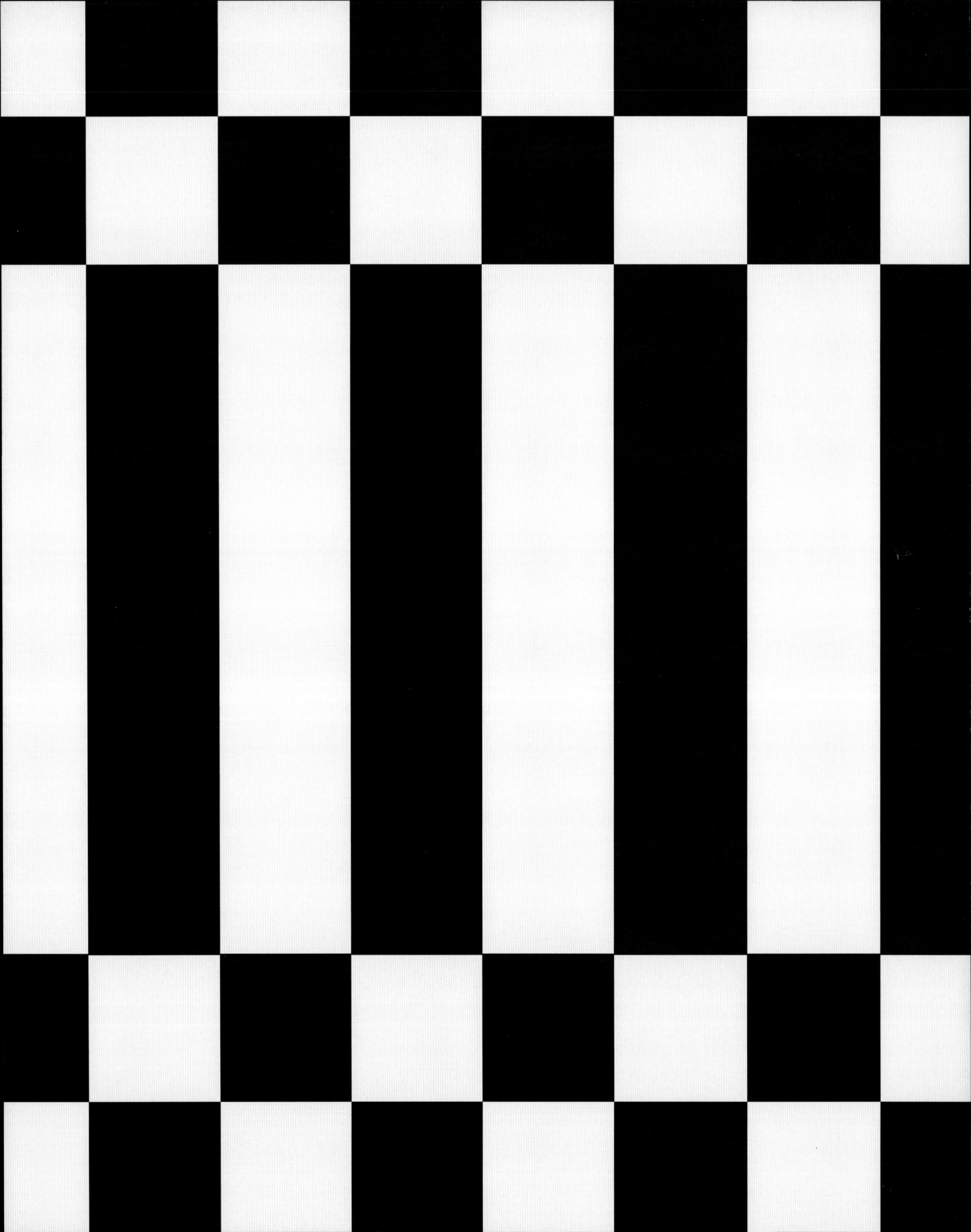

OFF *THE* WALL

In a house like this, you will never have enough eyes. The longer you look, the more you see. Frame watercolors, that poster from your favorite designer, or all your sketches. Then choose flowers and accessories that follow the colors and lines of what hangs on the wall. You'll keep looking around your own house.

VAN NATURE \ DE NATIONALE PARKEN VAN NEDERLAND
gestalten
THE HOME UPGRADE
IN PERFECT SHAPE FRITZ HANSEN

I AM
Kitchen Living
TRICIA GUILD KLEURENPALET
MODERNISTISCH
DESIGN
BARBER OSGERBY
ATLAS OF FURNITURE DESIGN
BARBER OSGERBY PROJECTS

HOCKNEY
PRADA
CATWALK
NADINE IJEWERE OUR OWN SELVES
PRESTEL

COCOA
& COFFEE

Soft, natural shapes in chocolate tones create warmth in the room and immediately set a mood. Minimalistically beautiful with a sleek sofa and designer lamps. Or rurally hospitable with Moroccan accessories and Berber rugs, and pots from Turkey. Choose what you like. With these colors, it will be cozy no matter what.

150 HOUSES
icons
THE SILVER SPOON CLASSIC
HIDE AND SEEK
THE HOME UPGRADE
Peter Lindbergh
Michelangelo
TASCHEN
gestalten

icons
icons by oscar
The works of photographer
Oscar Abolafia
TERRA
THE SILVER SPOON
CLASSIC
Abbas/Magnum

LAGUIOLE

THE DESIGN BOOK
Michelangelo
TASCHEN
AI WEIWEI
40
TASCHEN

Peter Lindbergh
RIHANNA
collage
THE HOME UPGRADE
Reebok

SUNNY **DELIGHT**

With bamboo, palm trees, various shades of orange, and furniture from the tropics, you bring summer into your home. Combine them with accessories from around the world, and you create a sun-drenched beach hut where everything is possible. And no matter the weather, the sun always shines in your home.

WAIKIKI BEACH
HAWAII

SURFERS PARADISE

ICONS

FERNANDES'
CHERRY
FERNANDES'
GREEN

MY ART BOOK OF LOVE
ICONS
TASCHEN
POWER OF MASKS
ARCHITECTURE BY WOMEN
Dominic Bradbury
Librero
Museum

HOCKNEY
PIET MONDRIAAN
TASCHEN
REMBRANDT
TASCHEN
CHARLES & RAY EAMES
TASCHEN
BON VOYAGE
Cabin Fever
THE SILVER SPOON CLASSIC

CLASSIC

THE SILVER SPOON CLASSIC
gestalten
Cabin Fever
Enchanting Cabins, Shacks, and Hideaways
BARBER OSGERBY PROJECTS

AM
12 06
KARLSSON
icons by oscar
FRANK BENNETT FISKE
titanen

Gijsbert Hanekroot

LET'S GET
LOUD

In an inspiring interior you will amaze yourself and others every day all over again. How do you achieve this? Combine classic items with new design and choose one or two bold colors. The result is funky and unconventional. Everyone will become cheerful, guaranteed. This works both at home and in the workplace. Give it a try!

HKliving lookbook
HKliving lookbook
YVES SAINT LAURENT
haute couture
CATWALK
The Ideal City
gestalten
STEFAN RAPPO
NUDE

SOMETHING'S
WOMAN MADE
HKliving lookbook

hkliving lookbook
YVES SAINT LAURENT
haute couture
CATWALK
The Ideal City
NUDE
STEFAN RAPPO

SOMETHING'S
OFF
"EVERYTHING I DO
IS FOR THE 17-YEAR-OLD
VERSION OF MYSELF."
VIRGIL ABLOH
TASCHEN
Jane Hall
WOMAN
MADE
GREAT WOMEN DESIGNERS
HKliving
lookbook
HK living

ROSE

THE OLDER THE BOLDER

IT GETS

A VISUAL PROTEST - THE ART OF BANKSY
The Ideal City

THE STORY OF ART
GOMBRICH
PHAIDON
The Metropolitan Museum of Art
Graphic
500 Designs that Matter
PHAIDON
PHAIDON
Ellen Mara De Wachter
TASCHEN
Thames & Hudson
BAUHAUS GOES WEST
MODERN ART AND DESIGN IN BRITAIN AND AMERICA
ALAN POWERS
MANIFESTO
UNAUTHORIZED & UNOFFICIAL
THE ART OF
BANKSY
A VISUAL PROTEST
PRESTEL
Tobias G. Natter (Ed.)
EGON SCHIELE
The Paintings
TASCHEN
HET NEDER-LANDSE

FLAVOUR

The Metropolitan Museum of Art
Art =
DRINK
HOCKNEY
A Chronology of Photography
PRESTEL
NADINE IJEWERE OUR OWN SELVES
Basquiat
The Ideal City
A VISUAL PROTEST THE ART OF BANKSY
NANOTECTURE TINY BUILT THINGS
PHOTO ICONS
MODERNE KUNST

DRINK
COOL!
THE EXPERTS' GUIDE TO THE BEST BARS IN THE WORLD
OTK
OTTOLENGHI TEST KITCHEN
JAPANEASY VEGAN
TIM ANDERSON
Tori Holmes
beauty water

ESCHER MEETS ISLAMIC ART
Willem Marinus Dudok
JUGENDSTIL
CHINESE PROPAGANDA POSTERS

ANNIE LEIBOVITZ AT WORK
gestalten
Petite Places
NADINE IJEWERE OUR OWN SELVES
PRESTEL
gestalten
Slow Escapes
HKliving lookbook

L'AMOUR
I'M SORRY
I DIDN'T MEAN
TO MAKE
THIS FACE
OUT LOUD

In the morning, you walk barefoot to the espresso machine. The tile floor feels cool. You can already smell the fresh bread. You don't need much for such a perfect start to the day. It can be very simple. Light and pure. When you see that everything is made with love and craftsmanship, it quickly feels like home.

ARTISAN *FOR LIFE*

WITTE CHOCOLADE FRAMBOZEN TAART

Suiker

UN CROISSANT

IF I DON'T
HAVE RED,
I USE BLUE

Pablo Picasso

EWISH
COOKBOOK
LEAH KOENIG
PHAIDON
icons
by oscar
icons by oscar
The works of photographer Oscar Abolafia
TERRA
The BARBER Book
PHAIDON
ATLAS OF FUR
ATLAS OF FURNITURE DESIGN

SALT

306
GAMBAS AL AJILLO I
CROQUETAS DE BACALAO I
CALAMARES II
ATÚN A LA BRASA
ZAMBURIÑAS II

YURRITA
ATÚN
CLARO
BALEA
SARDINAS (sardinillas)
EN ACEITE DE OLIVA
16/20 piezas • ELABORADO EN GALICIA
AZEITE OLIVE OLIVE OLIVENÖL
PEPUS
BONITO DEL NORTE EN ACEITE DE OLIVA
WHITE TUNA IN OLIVE OIL
CONSERVAS
YURRITA
1867
GASTRONOMIKA
8-12
SARDINILLAS
en aceite de oliva
sardinha
- em azeite -
Sardine in olive oil

BALEA
SARDINAS sardinillas
PEPUS

MORE INFO

you can find our
STORES in:

Amersfoort

Duiven

Maastricht

Sliedrecht

Zaandam

FOLLOW US
on social media

@Loods5

loods5.nl

COLOPHON

Uitgeverij Terra is part of Uitgeverij Lannoo nv
P.O. Box 23202
1100 DS Amsterdam
The Netherlands
terra@lannoo.nl
www.lannoo.com

Concept: Loods 5, Ontwerpstudio 5 (Annette Verkuijl and Brenda Braas)
Texts: Daniëlle van Hengst
Photography: Lotte van Uittert, Zoe Corbey, Riet Debruyne, Denise Pronk, Rogier Lulof
Interior styling & design: Ontwerpstudio 5
Proofreading: Barbara Luijken and Marijke Overpelt

First print, 2024

ISBN 9789020919547
NUR 454